# SHORT WALK
## MADE EASY

CW00395124

# CHILTERNS

Ordnance Survey

# Contents

## Walk 1

### PEGSDON HILLS

**Distance**
4 miles / 6.4km

**Time**
2½ hours

**Start/Finish**
¾ mile east of Pegsdon

**Parking** SG5 3JU
Hexton Road car
park, on B655, east of
Pegsdon

**Cafés/pubs**
The View, Pegsdon

Classic chalk
grassland, dry
valleys and rolling
downs nature
reserve

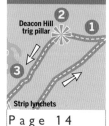

Deacon Hill
trig pillar

Strip lynchets

Page 14

## Walk 2

### DUNSTABLE DOWNS

**Distance**
2.75 miles / 4.4km

**Time**
1½ hours   CATCH A BUS

**Start/Finish**
Chilterns Gateway Centre

**Parking** LU6 2GY
Chilterns Gateway Centre National Trust car park

**Cafés/pubs**
View Café, Chilterns Gateway Centre

Gliders soaring over the downs, prehistoric track and Tree Cathedral

## Walk 3

### TRING RESERVOIRS

**Distance**
3.1 miles / 5 km

**Time**
1½ hours   CATCH A BUS

**Start/Finish**
Startop's End

**Parking** HP23 4LJ
Tring Reservoirs car park, Startop's End, Marsworth

**Cafés/pubs**
The Anglers Retreat and Waters Edge pubs

Canal and reservoir birdlife; an old toll house; waterside pubs

## Walk 4

### COOMBE HILL

**Distance**
2.5 miles / 4km

**Time**
1¼ hours

**Start/Finish**
Coombe Hill

**Parking** HP17 0UR
National Trust Coombe Hill car park

**Cafés/pubs**
Nearest in Wendover

Poignant memorial, extensive views and PM's country house

## Walk 5

### PENN WOOD

**Distance**
3 miles/4.8km

**Time**
1½ hours

CATCH A BUS

**Start/Finish**
Penn Street

**Parking** HP7 0PY
Woodland Trust Penn
Wood car park

**Cafés/pubs**
Penn Street

Glorious ancient
woodland for
year-round 'forest
bathing'

Page 42

## Walk 6

### CHRISTMAS COMMON

**Distance**
3.8 miles/6.1km

**Time**
2 hours

CATCH A BUS

**Start/Finish**
Watlington Hill

**Parking** OX49 5HS
National Trust
Watlington Hill car park

**Cafés/pubs**
Fox and Hounds,
Christmas Common

Stately beech
woods, a
charming village
and welcoming
pub

Page 48

## Walk 7

### HAMBLEDEN

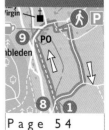

**Distance**
4.1 miles/6.6km

**Time**
2¼ hours

CATCH A BUS

**Start/Finish**
Hambleden

**Parking** RG9 6RP
Hambleden car park,
beside pub

**Cafés/pubs**
Hambleden and Aston

Beautiful stretch
of River Thames;
historic mill, lock
and church

Page 54

## Walk 8

RIVER THAMES AT COOKHAM

**Distance**
3.2 miles/5.2km

**Time**
1½ hours

**Start/Finish**
Cookham Moor

**Parking** SL6 9SB
National Trust
Cookham Moor car
park

**Cafés/pubs**
The Bounty, riverside at
Bourne End; Cookham

Thames Path,
riverside inn;
Cookham's art
and literary
associations

## Walk 9

HENLEY-ON-THAMES

**Distance**
3.5 miles/5.6km

**Time**
2 hours

**Start/Finish**
Henley-on-Thames

**Parking** RG9 1AY
Railway Station car
park

**Cafés/pubs**
Henley-on-Thames

Henley's regatta
course riverside,
Remenham
Woods and
church

## Walk 10

RIVER THAMES AT GORING

**Distance**
3 miles/4.8km

**Time**
1½ hours

**Start/Finish**
Goring

**Parking** RG8 9HB
Wheel Orchard car
park

**Cafés/pubs**
Goring

Superb 'Goring
Gap' countryside,
stately river and
lush meadows

# GETTING OUTSIDE IN THE CHILTERNS

**"**

... the Dunstable
Downs, where
you might see
wheeling red
kites and watch
gliders thermal
soaring

OS Champion
Karl Rushen

Dunstable Downs

A very warm welcome to the new Short Walks Made Easy guide to the Chilterns – what a fantastic selection of leisurely walks we have for you!

An Area of Outstanding Natural Beauty (AONB) covering 324 square miles and designated in 1965, the Chiltern Hills run south-west to north-east from Goring in Oxfordshire through Buckinghamshire and Bedfordshire to Hitchin in Hertfordshire, and are characterized by rolling downland, sweeping dry valleys and glorious beech woodlands. The Chilterns are bounded by the stately River Thames to the west and south.

You can explore the highest point in the Chilterns at Coombe Hill, rising to 852 feet above sea level. The views include the Prime Minister's country residence at Chequers. Walks visit other fine vantage points over the Oxfordshire Plain and Vale of Aylesbury from Watlington Hill and the Dunstable Downs, where you might see wheeling red kites and watch gliders thermal soaring.

Whether it's to see bluebells in spring, walk dappled sunlit glades enjoyed by speckled wood butterflies in summer or revel in the golden colours of autumn, the woodland walks at Penn Wood and from Christmas Common are a delight all year round.

The serene beauty of the Thames and its riverside make lovely days out in strolls from Hambleden, Cookham, Henley and Goring, while the Tring Reservoirs and Grand Union Canal offer locks, boats and welcoming towpath inns.

**Karl Rushen, OS Champion**

# WE SMILE MORE
# WHEN WE'RE OUTSIDE

Henley-on-Thames

Whether it's a short walk during our lunch break or a full day's outdoor adventure, we know that a good dose of fresh air is just the tonic we all need.

At Ordnance Survey (OS), we're passionate about helping more people to get outside more often. It sits at the heart of everything we do, and through our products and services, we aim to help you lead an active outdoor lifestyle, so that you can live longer, stay younger and enjoy life more.

We firmly believe the outdoors is for everyone, and we want to help you find the very best Great Britain has to offer. We are blessed with an island that is beautiful and unique, with a rich and varied landscape. There are coastal paths to meander along, woodlands to explore, countryside to roam, and cities to uncover. Our trusted source of inspirational content is bursting with ideas for places to go, things to do and easy beginner's guides on how to get started.

It can be daunting when you're new to something, so we want to bring you the know-how from the people who live and breathe the outdoors. To help guide us, our team of awe-inspiring OS Champions share their favourite places to visit, hints and tips for outdoor adventures, as well as tried and tested accessible, family- and wheelchair-friendly routes. We hope that you will feel inspired to spend more time outside and reap the physical and mental health benefits that the outdoors has to offer. With our handy guides, paper and digital mapping, and exciting new apps, we can be with you every step of the way.

**To find out more visit os.uk/getoutside**

## RESPECTING
## THE COUNTRYSIDE

You can't beat getting outside in the British countryside, but it's vital that we leave no trace when we're enjoying the great outdoors.

Let's make sure that generations to come can enjoy the countryside just as we do.

 Leave no trace

 Keep dogs under control; bin and bag waste

 Do not light fires; only BBQ at official sites

 Leave gates as you find them

 Keep to footpaths and open access land

 Plan ahead for your trip

For more details please visit
www.gov.uk/countryside-code

# USING THIS GUIDE

## Easy-to-follow Chilterns walks for all

### Before setting off

**Check the walk information panel to plan your outing**

- Consider using **Public transport** where flagged. If driving, note the satnav postcode for the car park under **Parking**
- The suggested **Time** is based on a gentle pace
- Note the availability of **Cafés**, tearooms and pubs, and **Toilets**

**Terrain and hilliness**

- **Terrain** indicates the nature of the route surface
- Any rises and falls are noted under **Hilliness**

**Walking with your dog?**

- This panel states where **Dogs** must be on a lead and how many stiles there are – in case you need to lift your dog
- Keep dogs on leads where there are livestock and between April and August in forest and on downland where there are ground-nesting birds

### A perfectly pocket-sized walking guide

- Handily sized for ease of use on each walk
- When not being read, it fits nicely into a pocket...
- ...so between points, put this book in the pocket of your coat, trousers or day sack and enjoy your stroll in glorious national park countryside – we've made it pocket-sized for a reason!

### Flexibility of route presentation to suit all readers

- **Not comfortable map reading?** Then use the simple-to-follow route profile and accompanying route description and pictures
- **Happy to map read?** New-look walk mapping makes it easier for you to focus on the route and the points of interest along the way
- **Read the insightful Did you know?, Local legend, Stories behind the walk** and **Nature notes** to help you make the most of your day out and to enjoy all that each walk has to offer

## OS information about the walk

• Many of the features and symbols shown are taken from Ordnance Survey's celebrated **Explorer** mapping, designed to help people across Great Britain enjoy leisure time spent outside

**OS information**

🏃 TL 132300
Explorer 193

• National Grid reference for the start point
• Explorer sheet map covering the route

## The easy-to-use walk map

• **Large-scale** mapping for ultra-clear route finding

• **Numbered points** at key turns along the route that tie in with the route instructions and respective points marked on the profile

• **Pictorial symbols** for intuitive map reading, see Map Symbols on the front cover flap

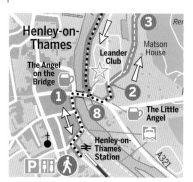

## The simple-to-follow walk profile

• Progress easily along the route using the illustrative profile, it has **numbered points** for key turning points and **graduated distance** markers

• Easy-read **route directions** with turn-by-turn detail

• Reassuring **route photographs** for each numbered point

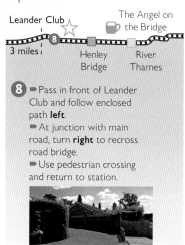

**8** ➥ Pass in front of Leander Club and follow enclosed path **left**.
➥ At junction with main road, turn **right** to recross road bridge.
➥ Use pedestrian crossing and return to station.

# PEGSDON HILLS

This lovely walk explores an outlier group of hills on the north-eastern tip of the Chilterns Area of Outstanding Natural Beauty. Dry valleys cut deeply into the north face of the Pegsdon Hills and the outlook from the path along the top of the escarpment is jaw-dropping in its reach. Not only does this area offer an interesting wildlife experience, with plants and insects typical of chalk country, but there's a lot of historical interest here too, ranging from the prehistoric to more modern.

## OS information

TL 132300
Explorer 193

**Distance**
4 miles/6.4km

**Time**
2½ hours

**Start/Finish**
Near Pegsdon

**Parking** SG5 3JU
Hexton Road car park on south side of B655, about ¾ mile east of Pegsdon

**Public toilets**
None

**Cafés/pubs**
The View (bar and restaurant), Pegsdon

**Terrain**
Field paths; open, rolling grassland; good tracks

**Hilliness**
Undulating with some short, steep sections

### Footwear

Winter/Spring/
Autumn ❄
Summer ☀

### Public transport
None

### Accessibility
〰〰〰〰〰〰〰
None for wheelchairs.
Suitable for all-terrain
pushchairs from **7** to
the end

### Dogs
Welcome but
keep on leads. No
stiles

**Did you know?** The ridge to the south of
Telegraph Hill is Lilley Hoo, home to a racecourse
in the 17th and 18th centuries. The first official
record of a race meeting is from September 1773
when a horse named Stripling won the Lilley Hoo
£50 stakes. It is said that King George IV was a
regular visitor and used the course to train his
racehorses.

**Local legend** In the 1820s, the nearby hamlet of
Lilley was home to Jonathan Kellerman, believed
by locals to be an alchemist. He supposedly had
a huge set of bellows in his outhouse and the
fumes from the furnace sometimes formed a
gigantic figure that hung in the air. Legend has it
that he disappeared without trace one day, the
furnace unlit and his house abandoned.

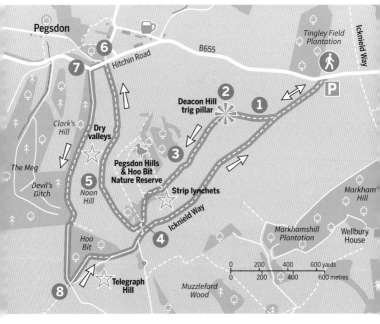

# STORIES BEHIND THE WALK

☆ **Trig pillar** At 564 feet above sea level, the trig pillar, or triangulation station, marks the highest point on Deacon Hill. Ordnance Survey trig pillars like this one started appearing in the British countryside in 1936. They were designed to hold the theodolites used by surveyors creating accurate maps of Great Britain. The view from the top includes parts of Bedfordshire and Cambridgeshire.

☆ **Dry valleys** Several short and steep-sided dry valleys cut into the escarpment of the Pegsdon Hills. While you'd normally expect to see streams or rivers running along the base of valleys, these ones are dry because the underlying bedrock (chalk) is highly permeable, so any water simply seeps through the soil. The valleys themselves were formed during the Ice Age when rain and melting snow, unable to penetrate the frozen ground, flowed over the surface.

Deacon Hill trig pillar

Dry valleys

**2** ½ mile **3** 1 m

Pegsdon Hills and Hoo Bit

🅿 Hexton Road car park

➡ Go through kissing-gate beside larger gate at end of car park.
➡ Walk with fence/hedgerow on left for 400 yards then swing **right** towards gate in fence.

**1** ➡ Go through gate and climb steep slope ahead on chalky path.
➡ Walk to trig pillar, hidden behind some shrubs.

**2** ➡ Turn your back on trig pillar and continue along edge of high ground, picking up faint trail that passes to **left** of solitary tree.
➡ Passing a hollow, trail descends but stays on hillside ledge to meet fence.

## ☆ Strip lynchets

Usually dating from medieval times or sometimes even earlier, strip lynchets, also known as cultivation terraces, were formed by soil drifting downhill when a slope was ploughed. The ridges of earth were often shaped into parallel terraces on the hillside, making cultivation easier. Many have since been ploughed over, although they are still clearly visible on Deacon Hill. Some sources suggest these ones were created in prehistoric times.

## ☆ Telegraph Hill

A wooden telegraph station was located on Telegraph Hill during the Napoleonic Wars. It was one of a line of beacons running from Great Yarmouth on the east coast of England to Admiralty House in London – partly following the Icknield Way. Telegraph Hill may also have been the site of a beacon during the Elizabethan era and during the English Civil War.

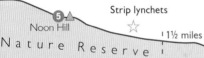

Strip lynchets
☆

Noon Hill    ⬆5️⃣    ı 1½ miles

N a t u r e    R e s e r v e   ı

6️⃣ 7️⃣
B655

3️⃣ ➡ Go through kissing-gate and follow trail across hillside as it dips and curves above trees to a fork in 300 yards.
➡ Bear **left** here, climbing. Path less clear at top of rise; make for fence and walk with it on left to kissing-gate.

4️⃣ ➡ Go through and keep **right**, beside fence on right.
➡ Turn sharp **right** at fence corner.
➡ Keep fence on right and continue for ¼ mile to the second kissing-gate.

# NATURE NOTES

The Pegsdon Hills form part of a nature reserve, known for the species that thrive on these open chalk grasslands. Among the plants found here are wild thyme, marjoram, wild basil, common rock-rose, harebell and woolly thistle. This thistle, only found on chalk and limestone soils, can be easily distinguished from other thistles by the cotton-like wool that covers part of the flowerhead. In spring, listen for skylarks singing and, come the autumn, watch for flocks of migrant fieldfare and redwing feeding on berries. Red kites can also often be seen.

The grassland is grazed by several species of native sheep to help control the spread of scrub. These include the Wiltshire horn, the Hebridean and the Herdwick, a hardy breed more commonly associated with the mountains of the Lake District.

After ❼, the route passes through and along the edge of woodland. Tree species here include sycamore, beech and holly.

Fieldfare

Telegraph Hill ☆

Clark's Hill ▲

2½ miles

❽

2 miles

🦆 Pegsdon Hills and Hoo Bit Nature Reserve

❺ ➡ Go through and begin steady descent.
➡ Pass through several more gates, following fence on right. When fence ends, keep **straight ahead** on clear path to bottom of slope.

❻ ➡ Go through gate, turn **left** along trail parallel with road.
➡ This emerges in rough layby in about 100 yards.

Common rock-rose

Herdwick sheep

Woolly thistle

Harebell

...niles

*Icknield Way*

3½ miles

4 miles

Hexton Road car park 🅿

**7** ➤ Turn **left** to pass beside large gate. Track heads uphill along woodland edge.
➤ At path junction near reserve entrance, veer slightly **right** on path marked by yellow-topped post and continue to next junction.

**8** ➤ Turn **sharp left**. Ignoring one path to right and reserve entrances on left, follow this track – Icknield Way – for 1¼ miles to return to parking area.

# DUNSTABLE DOWNS

CATCH A BUS

## OS information

TL 008195
Explorer 181

**Distance**
2.75 miles/4.4km

**Time**
1½ hours

**Start/Finish**
Chilterns Gateway
Centre

**Parking** LU6 2GY
National Trust pay-
and-display car park,
Chilterns Gateway
Centre, Whipsnade
Road, Dunstable (off
B4541)

**Public toilets**
Chilterns Gateway
Centre

**Cafés/pubs**
View Café, Chilterns
Gateway Centre

**Terrain**
Surfaced paths and
tracks; woodland
trails; meadows

**Hilliness**
Mostly flat with
some gentle
undulations

**Footwear**
Winter
Spring/Summer/
Autumn

Dunstable Downs form a long ridge of high ground – the highest in Bedfordshire – with far-reaching views over the surrounding countryside. After setting out from the National Trust's Chilterns Gateway Centre, this walk leaves the chalk escarpment and heads for Whipsnade, where walkers can visit the Tree Cathedral. Following the Icknield Way Trail for much of the time, you then make your way along a delightful path to emerge on the edge of the downs for an awesome stroll along the escarpment edge.

**Public transport**

The 'circular' number 40/40A bus from Dunstable runs Mon–Sat: centrebus. info

**Accessibility**

Wheelchairs on surfaced paths from ⓐ to ❷. Icknield Way is accessible in dry conditions and for robust chairs, albeit bumpy, from ❻ to end. Route suitable for all-terrain pushchairs

**Dogs**

Welcome but keep on leads. No stiles

**Did you know?** Dunstable Downs used to have an unusual Easter tradition. On Good Friday, local people would gather on the slopes above Pascombe Pit armed with oranges which they would then throw at each other. Many would race the rolling fruit, and children would often sell them on. The tradition stopped during World War II when oranges were hard to get hold of but resumed soon after. It stopped again in the late 1960s when health and safety considerations finally put an end to orange 'rolling' or 'pelting'.

**Local legend** The church of St Mary the Virgin at Church End, about a mile from Whipsnade, is said to be haunted by the headless ghost of a milkmaid. Wearing her yoke and pails, she follows a footpath from the north before entering the churchyard.

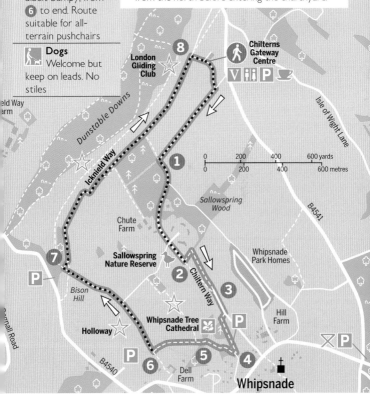

# STORIES BEHIND THE WALK

## ☆ Whipsnade Tree Cathedral

The Whipsnade Tree Cathedral was planted between 1930 and 1939 by Edmund Blyth. He had served in World War I and wanted to create a memorial to the friends he lost during the conflict. Aided by Albert Bransom, his plan was to plant trees, hedges and shrubs in the shape of a cathedral to create a legacy for his fallen comrades. The site is now maintained by the National Trust and is wheelchair accessible.

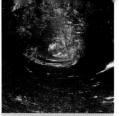

☆ **Holloway** The tree-fringed path joined at ⑥ is a holloway – a sunken lane that has been deepened by centuries of use and clearance. Using these ancient tracks is a delight, giving walkers the feeling of being totally cut off from the outside world. This one is believed to have been used since medieval times, linking the settlements of Whipsnade and Eaton Bray.

Chilterns Gateway Centre car park

① ½ mile

C h i l t e r n  W a

① 
➥ With your back to centre's main entrance, walk **straight ahead** – on surfaced path.
➥ At path junction in 80 yards, turn **right**.
➥ Turn **right** again along surfaced track to reach woodland.

➥ At woodland edge, go **left** along path.
➥ When path splits, bear **right**.
➥ After two black-and-white bollards, keep **straight ahead** along surfaced lane for 400 yards to signposted fence gap on left.

② ➥ Turn **left** through signposted gap to enter Wildlife Trust's Sallowsprings Reserve.
➥ A little way into meadow, follow grass trail round to **right** to re-meet the lane in 300 yards.

☆**Icknield Way** Stretching from East Anglia to Wiltshire, the Icknield Way is thought to be one of the oldest roads in Britain and was probably used for trading by ancient native British people. It is dotted with a wealth of archaeological sites and is also reputed to be haunted by a large black dog and a legion of Roman soldiers. Today, walkers can follow its route on a 170-mile long-distance path.

**Sallowsprings Nature Reserve**

☆ **London Gliding Club** The London Gliding Club was formed in 1930. Later that year, it moved to its current site at the foot of Dunstable Downs, an area that is perfect for catching the prevailing westerly winds. Many early gliding records were set at Dunstable, including ones for duration (22 hours, in 1937) as well as height (more than 14,000 feet set in 1939). Gliding was prohibited during World War II and the site became a prisoner of war camp.

**Whipsnade Tree Cathedral** ☆

2

3

1 mile

4 P Tree Cathedral car park

5

**3** ■ Turn **left** on rejoining lane.
■ Continue for 150 yards then take path on **right**, entering National Trust's Whipsnade land.
■ Gate leads into Tree Cathedral, but main route goes **left** before gate for 225 yards to wooden post-lined track.

**4** ■ After passing round side of gate, turn **right** along track.
■ Go through kissing-gate to enter Tree Cathedral. Keep **straight ahead**, between two parallel lines of trees to a bench.

# NATURE NOTES

The chalk slopes of Dunstable Downs are carefully managed by the National Trust to encourage wildflowers, birds and insects to thrive. From ❼ onwards, you'll see bird's-foot trefoil, ragwort, pyramidal orchid, bee orchid, bladder campion, common rock-rose, quaking grass and yellow rattle. In turn, these plants help to support populations of ground-nesting skylark, butterflies such as the Duke of Burgundy and chalk hill blue, and the red-and-black froghopper, the insect that creates the frothy mass known as cuckoo spit.

The woodland encountered along the way provides a colourful spectacle in the autumn and includes sycamore, horse chestnut, oak, beech, elder, hawthorn, hazel and wild cherry.

**Top**: red-and-black froghopper
**Above**: cuckoo spit
**Right**: quaking grass

Holloway ☆

❻ ┅┅┅┅┅┅
i 1½ miles

Icknield Way ☆

❼ ┅┅┅

2 miles i

Dunstabl

❺ ➥ Take grass path to **left** of bench. Leave Tree Cathedral by passing round side of redundant kissing-gate. Keep to left edge of field.
➥ Kissing-gate leads onto fenced path.

❻ ➥ Turn **right** at T-junction. Follow path for ½ mile.
➥ Go **straight** on emerging from trees and follow clearest path as it veers slightly **right** – on level ground – to reach gates.

Duke of Burgundy butterfly

Bird's-foot trefoil

Bladder campion

Ragwort

London Gliding Club ☆

Chilterns Gateway Centre

2½ miles

**Downs**

**7** ➡ Go through gate and walk with hedgerow on right. Keep to top edge of downs (all the way to **8**).

➡ Reaching fence corner with waymarker post beside it, keep **straight on**. After gate, continue in same direction.

**8** ➡ At next waymarker, swing up to **right** to return to start.

This page (clockwise): Marsworth Reservoir; bluebell wood, Christmas Common; Goring; Fawley Court, Henley-on-Thames
Opposite (clockwise): Grand Union canal; Goring; Church of St Mary the Virgin, Hambleden

# TRING
# RESERVOIRS

If you enjoy walking beside water or you're at all interested in wildlife, then you'll love this route. After admiring the colourful boats from the tranquil towpath of the Grand Union Canal, walk the Wendover Arm of this once-great waterway and then visit the reservoirs built to supply the waterways. The reedbeds, woodland and reservoirs themselves are home to a wide range of bird species including many types of duck and geese and, in winter, the rare bittern.

## OS information

🚶 SP 919140
Explorer 181

**Distance**
3.1 miles/5km

**Time**
1½ hours

**Start/Finish**
Startop's End,
Marsworth

**Parking** HP23 4LJ
Canal & River Trust's
Tring Reservoirs
pay-and-display car
park, Lower Icknield
Way, Startop's End,
off B489

**Public toilets**
None

**Cafés/pubs**
Waters Edge and
Anglers Retreat
pubs, both at
Startop's End

**Terrain**
Canal towpaths,
including one short,
very narrow section
with a drop to the
water on one side;
reservoir paths

**Hilliness**
Flat apart from
where bridges are
encountered

43

**Did you know?** Canals played an important role in the Industrial Revolution – although the creation of the Grand Union Canal, linking several existing waterways, dates from a later period. Horse-drawn transport couldn't cope with the quantities of goods being produced, or the raw materials being moved around, so engineers built man-made waterways. Canals had their drawbacks though, including lack of speed, and they couldn't compete with the railways from the mid-19th century onwards.

**Local legend** The last witch to be ducked in England was Ruth Osborne, from nearby Long Marston. In 1751, after rumours that she had cursed a farmer who had refused to give her some buttermilk, a mob gathered in Tring demanding to know the whereabouts of Ruth and her husband. The couple were eventually handed over, tied up and thrown into the local pond. Ruth reportedly died minutes after being hauled back onto the bank.

**Footwear**
Year round 👟

🚍 **Public transport**
Bus service 61, Aylesbury to Dunstable, stops in Marsworth, ½ mile from 🚶: redeagle. org.uk

♿ **Accessibility**
Robust all-terrain wheelchairs and pushchairs as far as ③

🐕 **Dogs**
Welcome but keep on leads. No stiles

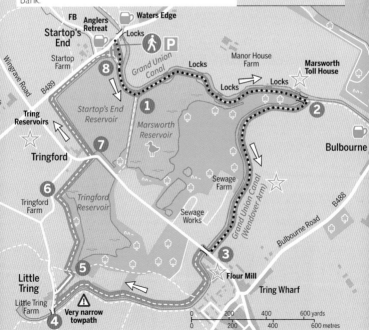

Startop's End · FB · Anglers Retreat · 🅿 Waters Edge · Locks
Wingrave Road · B489 · Startop Farm
Grand Union Canal · Locks · Manor House Farm · **Marsworth Toll House** ⭐
Locks · Locks ②
⑧ · Startop's End Reservoir · Marsworth Reservoir
**Tring Reservoirs** ⭐
**Tringford**
⑦
① 
Bulbourne ☕
⑥ · Tringford Farm · Tringford Reservoir
Sewage Farm
Grand Union Canal (Wendover Arm) ⭐
Sewage Works
⑤ · B488 · Bulbourne Road
**Little Tring** · Little Tring Farm · ④ · ⚠ **Very narrow towpath**
③ · ⭐ **Flour Mill** · **Tring Wharf**
0  200  400  600 yards
0  200  400  600 metres

# STORIES BEHIND THE WALK

☆ **Tring Reservoirs** Constructed between 1802 and 1816, Tring Reservoirs were created to supplement the water in the Grand Union Canal. There was insufficient water available from Tring summit so the reservoirs were needed to facilitate proper operation of the locks. The largest of the four, Wilstone Reservoir, has a capacity of 240 million imperial gallons.

☆ **Marsworth Toll House** Tolls were charged on many English canals with toll houses situated at major junctions and on some locks. The unusual triangular structure on the Marsworth Toll House – a little like a bay window – would have allowed the toll-keeper a view up and down the canal. The building featured in the 1964 film *The Bargee* starring Harry H Corbett and Ronnie Barker.

🍵 The Anglers Retreat

🍵 Waters Edge

Lock ... Lock ... Lock ... Lock ... Lock ... Lock ... Lock ... Lock

**G r a n d   U n i o n   C a n a l**

1½ mile

Marsw Toll H

**P**

Tring Reservoirs car park

➠ Go through gate at far end of car park.

➠ Keep **right** at early fork, soon walking with Startop's End Reservoir on right. Continue to next fork.

**1** ➠ At split, turn **left**, walking beside canal for almost ⅔ mile to bridge.

☆ **Wendover Arm** Linking Bulbourne in Hertfordshire with Wendover in Buckinghamshire, this short arm of the Grand Union Canal opened in 1799. Most of it has been unnavigable since the end of the 19th century, but the Wendover Canal Trust has been gradually restoring it, reopening an initial section in 2005. The charity aims to reopen the whole canal, and restore the towpath in its entirety, by 2030.

☆ **Flour mill**

Flour has been milled at Tring Wharfe since the start of the 19th century. It was originally the site of a water mill, but this was replaced by a windmill in 1875. As steam-powered mills became more profitable and could produce finer flour, windmilling became obsolete, and the windmill was demolished in about 1911. The Heygate family bought the site in 1944 and today the mill is fully automated, producing more than 12 tonnes of flour per hour.

Flour mill ☆

1 mile ❙        ③    1½ miles ❙

☆ **W e n d o v e r    A r m**

**②** ▶ After crossing bridge over canal's Wendover Arm, turn **sharp left** to pass back under it.
▶ Walk with Wendover Arm on right for more than ½ mile to road bridge.

**③** ▶ Go through gate, turn **right** to cross road bridge.
▶ Immediately go **left** to rejoin towpath, now with canal on left, to next road bridge.

# NATURE NOTES

With reedbeds, wet woodland and open water, the reservoirs provide a number of habitats for a variety of birds. The area is particularly well known for its winter wildfowl, including wigeon, pochard, teal, tufted duck and nationally important numbers of shoveler. Geese and ducks are present all year, though, and you'd be unlucky not to see Canada geese, coots, greylag geese, mallards and black-headed gulls.

Rare bitterns, known for their booming calls, feed in the reedbeds between December and February. Come the spring, you might even hear a cuckoo in this area as well as large numbers of breeding reed and sedge warblers.

Trees fringing the canal towpaths include ash, sycamore, whitebeam and horse chestnut. Visit in late summer to forage for blackberries (bramble), elderberries and sloe berries (blackthorn).

Sloes

very narrow towpath

☆ W e n d o v e r   A r m

⚠

Steps

4

2 miles

5

**4** ➠ **Climb** steps to right of bridge.
➠ Turn **right** along road for 90 yards.
➠ Just after houses, take Tringford Pumping Station's access track on **right**, continuing to fingerposted junction.

**5** ➠ As track bends right, enter private parking area on **left** and bear **left** along path through trees to next path junction in ¼ mile.

**Above:** greylag goose
**Below:** bittern

**Top:** sedge warbler
**Above:** southern hawker dragonfly

6
2½ miles

7

8
3 miles
Tring Reservoirs car park

**7** ▸ Cross diagonally **left** to join path beside Startop's End Reservoir (water on right).
▸ Keep to reservoir edge as it bends **right** and continue to next corner.

▸ Bear **right** when path splits.
▸ Walk beside Tringford Reservoir until you reach road.

**8** ▸ Here, descend steps on **left** to return to car park.

# WALK 4

# COOMBE HILL

As befits the highest point in the Chilterns – 853 feet above sea level – the views from the memorial on Coombe Hill are truly magnificent. After heading out to the summit on a wheelchair-friendly path, this figure-of-eight walk then continues along the top of the escarpment, allowing opportunities to soak up this amazing outlook as well as enjoy the birds, plants and insects typical of chalk country. The return route uses a track flanked by grand old beech trees.

### OS information

🧭 SP 851062
Explorer 181

**Distance**
2.5 miles / 4 km

**Time**
1¼ hours

**Start/Finish**
Coombe Hill

**Parking** HP17 0UR
National Trust's
Coombe Hill car
park, Lodge Hill,
Ellesborough; 3 miles
west of Wendover

**Public toilets**
None

**Cafés/pubs**
Wendover; ice cream
van often in car park

**Terrain**
Surfaced path;
woodland trails and
tracks; rougher paths
across grassland and
scrubland

**Hilliness**
Flat until ❸, then
mostly gently
undulating but
with short, steeper
slopes at ❹ and on
descent to ❼

**Did you know?** When Arthur and Ruth Lee gifted Chequers in trust to the nation in 1917, they also donated the 106 acres of the estate at Coombe Hill to the National Trust. The conservation charity, which was formed in 1895, has managed it ever since.

**Local legend** One of the attic rooms at Chequers is said to be haunted by Lady Mary Grey who, like her more famous sister Lady Jane Grey, had a claim to the English throne. Seeing her as a potential threat, Elizabeth I kept her under house arrest at Chequers for two years. She slept in one of the attic rooms at the mansion. Among those who claim to have 'sensed something weird' while staying in the attic is Bea Gove, daughter of Conservative politician Michael Gove.

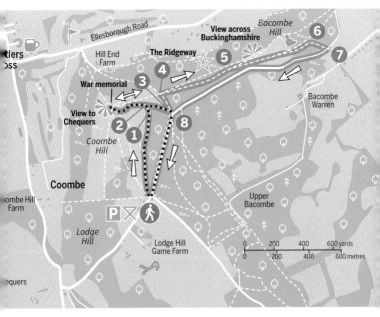

# STORIES BEHIND THE WALK

⚜ **War memorial** The memorial on Coombe Hill was one of the first ever built in Britain to honour the dead from a conflict rather than to commemorate a victory. It remembers the 148 men from Buckinghamshire who died during the Second Boer War. Erected in 1908, it was almost destroyed by lightning in 1938 and also suffered lightning damage in the 1990s. In 2010 substantial restoration work was completed by Buckinghamshire County Council; the memorial was rededicated, and two previously omitted names were added.

⚜ **Buckinghamshire** Extensive views over Buckinghamshire, including the Vale of Aylesbury, come and go as the walk makes its way from the memorial on Coombe Hill along the top of the escarpment. Including Milton Keynes, its largest settlement and only city, the population of the ceremonial county was estimated to be just over 800,000 at the start of the 2020s.

View
War        Chequ·
memorial    ⚜

Coombe  Hill                    ¦ ½ mile

P Coombe Hill car park

⮞ Standing at car park entrance, facing road, go through gate on **right**.
⮞ Keep **straight ahead** on broad, level path with fence on right for ⅓ mile.

**1** ⮞ Path swings **left**, away from fence, and continues to war memorial.
⮞ From war memorial, retrace steps for 250 yards to where surfaced path swings right.

**2** ⮞ Leave surfaced path here to keep **straight ahead** on grass, aiming for two wooden posts about 40 yards away. Faint path starts here and leads towards a fenced woodland.

**Chequers** Chequers, visible from the memorial, down in the valley to the left, is the country house of Britain's Prime Minister. The current house was constructed in 1565 but it is believed there was a building on the site as early as the 11th century. The house was gifted to the nation by owners Arthur and Ruth Lee towards the end of World War I for the Prime Minister to use as a relaxing country retreat and as a venue to entertain foreign dignitaries.

### ☆ The Ridgeway

This 87-mile waymarked, long-distance path runs from near the massive stone circle at Avebury in Wiltshire to Ivinghoe Beacon in the Chilterns. For much of its distance, it follows an ancient thoroughfare used by prehistoric traders, invading armies and medieval herdsman to cross the chalk uplands of southern England. It is one of 16 National Trails in England and Wales.

The Ridgeway

1 mile

**3** ▪ At woodland edge, go through **left-hand** of two gates.
▪ Turn sharp **left**, walking downhill beside fence on left to next junction.

**4** ▪ After 150 yards, turn **right** at path crossing – signposted The Ridgeway. Follow path out of woods and across scrubland.
▪ Keep **right** at fork soon after information panel – on higher, clearer path – eventually reaching metal kissing-gate.

# NATURE NOTES

This walk passes through a number of habitats, each giving rise to different species. You'll find gorse, hawthorn, bramble and even juniper on the scrubland on Coombe Hill's summit plateau, while the rare chalk grassland is home to fragrant orchids, bee orchids, clustered bellflowers, harebells, common rock-rose and wild thyme. Among the butterflies found here are the chalk hill blue, brown argus, marbled white and meadow brown.

Between **5** and **6**, watch for small mounds covering parts of the open grassland. These are anthills created by the yellow meadow ant, a creature that spends most of its life underground.

In autumn, fieldfare and redwing feed on the berries that grow on the trees and shrubs along the grassland edge. These include buckthorn, spindle and dogwood. The more dense woodland is home to oak, beech, ash, birch and holly.

**Above**: juniper berries
**Below**: brown
argus butterfly

View across
Buckinghamshire

Anthills   Bacombe Hill

☆ T h e   R i d g e w a y   1½ miles   **6**   **7**

**5** ► 40 yards after kissing-gate, bear **right** at faint fork – on higher, less clear path.
► At another fork, keep **right** again.
► Path descends. Follow it to substantial marker post.

**6** ► Just before short rise, turn sharp **right** at an Aylesbury Outer Ring waymarker.
► Descending through trees, keep **left** at next waymarker.
► Trail shortly drops to gate leading onto a crossing track.

Yellow meadow ant mounds

**Above**: marbled white butterfly
**Below**: dogwood

2½ miles

**8**

Coombe Hill car park 🅿 ⛌

2 miles

**7** ➡ Turn **right** along track.
➡ Follow it for ⅔ mile, to arrive at gate on right where walk entered woods at **3**.

**8** ➡ Don't go through the gate; instead swing **left** to walk with fence on right.
➡ Path returns to car park in ⅓ mile.

Opposite (clockwise): cattle at
Cock Marsh; red kite; bramble
flowers; roe deer
This page (clockwise):
white admiral butterfly;
meadow cranesbill; bullfinch

41

# WALK 5

## PENN WOOD

CATCH A BUS

**OS information**

⊕ SU 923962
Explorer 172

**Distance**
3 miles/4.8km

**Time**
1½ hours

**Start/Finish**
Penn Street

**Parking** HP7 0PY
Woodland Trust
Penn Wood car park,
beside Holy Trinity
Church, Penn Street

**Public toilets**
None

**Cafés/pubs**
The Squirrel and The
Hit or Miss pubs in
Penn Street

**Terrain**
Woodland paths,
some surfaced,
occasionally grassy

**Hilliness**
Level apart from
slight dip and climb
towards end

**Footwear**
Winter 🥾
Spring/Summer/
Autumn 👞

Penn Wood is one of the largest areas of ancient woodland in the Chilterns, containing some broadleaf trees that are two or three centuries old. Whatever time you visit – even in the depths of winter – wandering its many tracks and trails provides an opportunity to get closer to nature. Once part of a massive area of common land, Penn Wood has a fascinating history too, with earthworks hidden among the trees as well as pits where chalk, clay and flint would once have been extracted.

**Public transport**
Bus 1/1A, High
Wycombe to Hemel
Hempstead, stops on
A404, ¼ mile from ⓚ:
carouselbuses.co.uk

**Accessibility**
Wheelchair friendly
to ❶, and ❼ to end;
plus, in dry conditions,
for robust, all-terrain
chairs that can cope
with some exposed
tree roots, from ❶
to the kissing-gate
midway between ❷
and ❸

**Dogs**
Welcome. No
stiles

**Did you know?** The Woodland Trust, which
owns Penn Wood, started life in Devon in 1972
when a group of friends got together to protect
some local ancient woodland. Today, it has half
a million members and supporters, and cares
for more than 1,000 areas of public woodland
containing at least 50 million trees.

**Local legend** David Blakely, murdered by Ruth
Ellis – the last woman to be hanged in the
UK – is buried in the graveyard of Holy Trinity
Church in the neighbouring village of Penn. In
the 1980s a ghostly figure of a woman in white
was seen leaving the churchyard. Some like to
believe this was the ghost of Ruth Ellis pining
for her former lover.

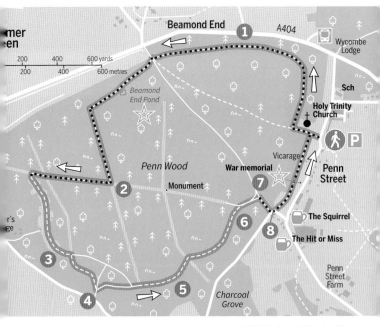

**Walk 5** Penn Wood   **43**

# STORIES BEHIND
# THE WALK

✝ **Holy Trinity Church** Built in 1849 by the first Earl Howe, Holy Trinity Church at Penn Street began life as a chapel of ease to Holy Trinity Church in the neighbouring village of Penn. The chancel is reserved for the use of the Howe family, who still live at Penn House. The north-west end of the churchyard, containing the tomb of the third earl and his wife, has its own lychgate and separate avenue of approach.

☆ Ownership

Up until the Enclosure Acts, Penn Wood had been used for communal grazing. In 1855, though, ownership passed to the first Earl Howe. For many years, local people protested and tried to reclaim the land they said was theirs. Only in 1999 was public access restored, when the Woodland Trust bought the site to prevent it from being turned into a golf course.

✝ Holy Trinity Church

🅿 Penn Wood car park

½ mile

➡ With your back to church gates, turn **right** along surfaced path – signposted Penn Woods short trail.
➡ After 100 yards, take path on **right**.
➡ Keep to path as it bends **left** after 300 yards; continue to crossways.

**1** ➡ Go **straight over** at crossing of routes.
➡ At next junction, cross diagonally **left**.
➡ Keep to clearest path as it makes sweeping bend **left** then runs arrow-straight for ¼ mile to intersection.

## ☆ Chair making

Dancer and Hearne, the chair manufacturer, started in a workshop behind the Hit or Miss pub in Penn Street in the 1890s. Using timber, particularly beech, from local woods, it grew to be one of the largest chair makers in Europe, producing nearly half a million annually. During World War II, the Penn Street site was used for the production of parts for the De Havilland Mosquito fighter-bomber. After the war, Dancer and Hearne mainly produced chairs for schools but, after a takeover by Parker Knoll and a move to plastic chairs in schools, the business closed in 1970.

## ☆ War memorial

The war memorial remembering local men killed in World War I, paid for by public donations, was unveiled in June 1922. During World War II soldiers from much further afield were trained in Penn Wood when the Tyneside Survey Regiment established a training camp here. Troops from the USA and Canada were among those based at the camp. At the end of the war, it was used as a reception centre for former prisoners of war returning to Britain.

Beamond ☆   1 mile                                    1½ miles
End Pond

**2** ⮕ At next crossing (grassier than previous ones), go **right**.
⮕ In ¼ mile, about 100 yards after trail joins from left, turn **left** on path through bracken.
⮕ Use kissing-gate and swing **left** across open area for ¼ mile to re-enter woods.

**3** ⮕ Less than 100 yards into the trees, path joins from left at waymarker post. Route ahead immediately splits. Bear **right** here, bending **right** with track towards gate.

# NATURE NOTES

Penn Wood is dominated by beech, oak and birch, although you'll spot other tree species here too, including rowan, holly, elder and some conifers such as Douglas fir. Autumn is a great time to visit, with the beech trees in particular putting on a fine display of colour and the holly and rowan bearing bright berries. Springtime sees the woodland floor covered with primroses and bluebells. Bracken thrives in more open areas in summer, turning a coppery colour in the autumn. Watch for muntjac and roe deer as well as a wide range of woodland birds such as brambling and jay, and butterflies like the speckled wood and, in July and August, white admiral.

The woods also contain a number of small ponds, one of which – Beamond End Pond – is passed between ❶ and ❷. These provide a home for various amphibians and invertebrates like the broad-bodied chaser dragonfly.

Bracken fronds in autumn

❸

¦ 2 miles

❹

❺ ➤ Bear **left** when path forks in open area.
➤ Go through gate at path crossing.
➤ Route meanders; follow Penn and Common Woods long trail for 400 yards until path joins from left at marker post.

❹ ➤ Immediately before gate on woodland edge, turn **left** – up short slope, soon walking with fence on right.
➤ Keep **straight on**, through gate to next path split.

Muntjac

Beech leaves

Broad-bodied
chaser dragonfly

War memorial ☆

⑥ 2½ miles

⑦ ⑧

3 miles 🅿

The Squirrel ☕

The Hit or Miss ☕

Penn Wood
car park

➡ Swing **right** on
joining path from left.
➡ Go through
kissing-gate.
➡ Keep **straight
ahead** on joining
clear path from left
to next junction
(waymarker post) in
125 yards.

⑦ ➡ Turn **right** at
junction with
broader path.
➡ Leave woods at
gate and turn **left**
along lane (pubs to
right).

⑧ ➡ Go immediately
**left** again – along
edge of village green.
➡ Keep close to
trees on left, later
passing through
short section of
woodland to return
to car park.

**Walk 5** Penn Wood  **47**

# CHRISTMAS
# COMMON

This walk starts from Watlington Hill, one of the highest parts of the Chilterns. Enjoying occasional far-reaching views over the Oxford plain, it enters the charmingly named hamlet of Christmas Common before heading through stately beech woods and out along an old lane. The soft, gently rolling nature of the Chiltern Hills is experienced as the walk briefly crosses open fields before re-entering dense woodland. It then returns to the hamlet where, if you've timed things right, refreshments await in a delightful country pub.

| OS information | |
|---|---|
| 🏃 SU 709935 Explorer 171 | |
| **Distance** 3.8 miles/6.1km | |
| **Time** 2 hours | |
| **Start/Finish** Watlington Hill | |
| **Parking** OX49 5HS National Trust Watlington Hill car park, Hill Road, near Christmas Common | |
| **Public toilets** None | |
| **Cafés/pubs** Fox and Hounds, Christmas Common | |
| **Terrain** Quiet roads, tracks, field and woodland paths | |
| **Hilliness** Mostly gently undulating apart from steep descent on approaching ➎ | |
| **Footwear** Winter 👢 Spring/Summer/ Autumn 👟 | |

**Did you know?** A lot of the woodland on this
walk is managed by Forestry England. Formerly
known as the Forestry Commission, this public
body was established to rebuild and maintain a
strategic timber reserve after the trench warfare
of World War I left woodland resources severely
depleted. The Forestry Act came into force on
September 1, 1919 and the new commission was
given a lot of freedom to acquire and plant land.
Agriculture was depressed in the 1920s so it was
able to buy land cheaply.

**Local legend** There is some doubt about the age
and original intentions of the 'White Mark' cut
into the chalk of Watlington Hill. Some theories
suggest our ancestors created it many centuries,
if not millennia ago as a phallic symbol. Whether
or not this is true, what is known is that it
was 'modified' in 1764 by local squire Edward
Horne who wanted to create the illusion that
Watlington parish church had a spire.

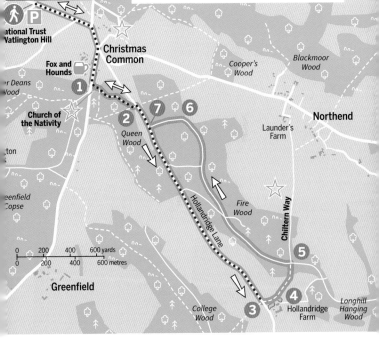

# STORIES BEHIND THE WALK

☆ **Christmas Common**  There are several theories about how the hamlet of Christmas Common got its name. It may be because of the holly coppices found here, or it may have been named after a local family. A more likely theory relates to the Civil War. In the Christmas of 1643, the Parliamentarians held nearby Watlington while the Royalists defended the ridge. Because it was Christmas a temporary truce was called and both armies met at Christmas Common during the festivities.

## National Trust at Watlington Hill

The National Trust has owned parts of the Watlington Hill Estate since the Esher family, who bought it in 1920, made their first donation to the charity in 1941. Further gifts of land followed, and the trust bought the last part of Watlington Hill in the early 1990s. Today, the 111-acre estate is managed by trust staff and the local volunteer group, The Friends of Watlington Hill, who meet monthly to carry out conservation tasks.

Christmas Common ☆

Church of the Nativity

National Trust at Watlington Hill

Fox and Hounds

½ mile

Queen Wood

H o l

**P** Watlington Hill car park

**1** ➡ Leave car park and turn **right** along road.
➡ Turn **right** again at T-junction, walking on grass verge.
➡ As one road goes left, keep **right** – signposted Nettlebed and Henley – towards pub.

**1** ➡ Less than 100 yards after passing Fox and Hounds pub, turn **left** along path to right of housing access drive.
➡ Entering woods go **straight over** crossing of paths, following white arrows on trees to the end of the woodland.

## ☆ Church of the Nativity

Soon after ❶ and before entering Queen Wood, watch for gravestones through a gap on the right. In keeping with the Christmas Common name, this is the graveyard of the Church of the Nativity. Built in 1889 as a chapel of ease, it became redundant in the 20th century and is now a private home – complete with the unusual garden seen from the path.

## ☆ Chiltern Way

This 134-mile long-distance circular path takes in many of the highlights of the Chilterns Area of Outstanding Natural Beauty. Since it opened in 2000, three extensions have been created, adding a further 90 miles to the total distance. The route is managed by the volunteers of the Chiltern Society, a charity set up to protect and promote the area's landscape, environment and human heritage.

d r i d g e  L a n e

1 mile

1½ miles

Hollandridge Farm

❷ ➡ Emerging from woods, go **left** along gravel drive and then turn **right** along lane.
➡ Go **straight over** crossing of routes (barriers to left and right) following lane for almost 1 mile to wide field gates on left before Hollandridge Farm.

❸ ➡ Go **left** to pass round side of farm gates.
➡ Walk beside trees on right for 125 yards to reach waymarked post.

# NATURE NOTES

The woodland encountered on this walk is typical of the mixed woods found throughout the Chilterns, containing a variety of trees and shrubs including beech, oak, holly, bramble, rowan, ash, field maple and elder. In late spring and early summer, elder is covered in the creamy-coloured flower clusters used to make a fragrant cordial. Later in the summer, these give way to dark purple berries, good for making wine. Watch too for various fungi on the woodland floor, such as chanterelle and shaggy parasol, and on tree trunks, like beefsteak fungus (particularly in late summer, autumn and early winter).

In summer, the verges of Hollandridge Lane are home to various plants including nettle, rosebay willowherb and burdock. Burdock seeds, or burrs, are said to have inspired the Swiss engineer George de Mestral to invent Velcro. This happened in 1941 after he'd been out hunting in the Alps, and noticed that his dog's coat was covered in burrs.

**Top**: chanterelle
**Above**: shaggy parasol

Chiltern Way

☆    ¦ 2 miles     F i r e    W o o d     ¦ 2½ miles

**5**

**4** ➡ As indicated by waymarkers, turn **left** on faint path through middle of field — gently downhill.
➡ Path enters woods at Oxfordshire Way/Chiltern Way signpost.
➡ Descend steeply into woods for 100 yards to track junction.

**5** ➡ At crossing of routes turn **left** along track.
➡ When route ahead splits in ⅓ mile, keep **right**, on lower path all the way to edge of wood.

Burdock seeds, or burrs

**Top**: acorn
**Above**: elderberries

Church of    Christmas
the Nativity    Common      National Trust at
   ☆     ☕ ☆     Watlington Hill

**7**    Queen Wood    Fox and    3½ miles   Watlington   **P**
3 miles          Hounds         Hill car park

**6** ➥ Nearing wooden fence on woodland edge, keep **straight ahead** and then quickly swing slightly **left** as indicated by white arrow on tree.
➥ Head gently uphill to emerge on Hollandridge Lane.

**7** ➥ Turn **right** for 175 yards to **2**, there going **left** to retrace steps to car park.

# HAMBLEDEN

CATCH A BUS

This walk starts from the gorgeous Buckinghamshire village of Hambleden, graced by idyllic brick-and-flint cottages and one of the prettiest churches in the region. Tracks, field paths and quiet lanes lead down to an old mill beside a particularly beautiful stretch of the River Thames, crossed by pedestrians via a bridge and a lock gate. A short loop, one of two on this walk, then calls in at the hamlet of Aston, and the chance for refreshments at the pub, before the return to Hambleden.

| OS information |
|---|
| SU 784865 Explorer 171 |

| **Distance** |
|---|
| 4.1 miles/6.6 km |

| **Time** |
|---|
| 2¼ hours |

| **Start/Finish** |
|---|
| Hambleden |

| **Parking** RG9 6RP |
|---|
| Pay-and-display car park beside Stag and Huntsman pub, Hambleden |

| **Public toilets** |
|---|
| In car park on Skirmett Road, 100 yards off route near ➋ |

| **Cafés/pubs** |
|---|
| Stag and Huntsman pub, Hambleden; Flower Pot pub, Aston |

| **Terrain** |
|---|
| Rough tracks, field paths, pavement, riverside meadow, surfaced lanes |

**Hilliness**
Barely noticeable descent and ascent to and from river

**Footwear**
Spring/Autumn/Winter 🥾 Summer 👟

**Public transport**
Bus service 850, Reading to High Wycombe, stops on the A4155, close to ③: arrivabus.co.uk/beds-and-bucks/

**Accessibility**
Wheelchairs: use ♿ as far as River Thames at ④. Suitable for all-terrain pushchairs from ➌ until the lock just after ④

**Dogs**
Welcome but keep on leads. No stiles

**Local legend** When the Roman villa at Hambleden was excavated in 1912, archaeologists discovered the remains of 97 new-born babies in the grounds. The shocking number of burials and the fact that most of the babies died at roughly the same age has led to speculation that they were the victims of infanticide. We'll probably never know.

**Did you know?** WH Smith, the newspaper wholesaler and founder of the retail chain named after him, was a churchwarden at St Mary the Virgin in Hambleden and played the organ there as a hobby. There is a small brass plaque dedicated to him on the nave's south wall.

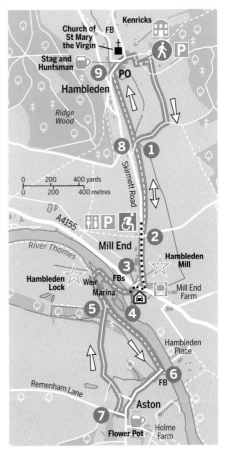

# STORIES BEHIND
# THE WALK

☆ **Hambleden Mill** Although the oldest part of the current building dates from the late 18th century, there is a record of a mill at Hambleden in the Domesday Book of 1086. During the 19th century, it supplied flour to Huntley & Palmers, the biscuit manufacturer, in nearby Reading. Every week, a barge called *Maid of the Mill* would take flour upstream to the biscuit factory which exported products all over the world.

☆ **Hambleden Lock** Before the first pound lock was built at Hambleden in 1773, a flash lock existed to help those navigating the River Thames. This involved a single gate consisting of upright boards, known as paddles, which would be removed to allow boats to be carried downstream on a 'flash' of water. Upstream traffic would be winched or towed through the lock. The current lock was last rebuilt in 1994.

Skirmett Road car
(100 yards right

🥤 Stag and Huntsman

🚶 🏠 Kenricks

🅿 Hambleden car park

➡ Walk through gap beside gate at car park's far end. Turn sharp **left**, across recreation area.

➡ Pass through narrow gap in trees ahead and turn **right** along track.

➡ At T-junction of track, turn **right** to kissing-gate in 300 yards.

① ½ mile

① ➡ Go through metal kissing-gate on **left**.

➡ Walk along **right-hand** edge of field (faint path). Go through kissing-gate beside larger gate in far corner to reach lane.

② 🅿 🚻 1

② ➡ Cross minor road and continue on pavement in same direction.

➡ Turn **right** at T-junction with A4155 and walk along pavement for 70 yards to fingerpost opposite.

## ⌂ Kenricks

Kenricks was built as a rectory in 1725, on the site of the original manor house. The Rev. Scawen Kenrick had a Baroque-style frontage added to the medieval building. This rather grand, west-facing façade is what walkers can see as they make their way back across the last field near the end of the walk. Various outbuildings include a dovecot and stables dating from 1680.

## † ■ Church of St Mary the Virgin

St Mary's in Hambleden has a long history, and the building and its contents reflect this. The main door dates from the 14th century, the altar incorporates a 16th-century carved wooden panel, while the oldest part of the existing structure is the north transept, which was built in about 1230. Older still is the stone font near the main door. Some sources say this is one of the last remnants of the original Saxon church, potentially predating the Norman church by several centuries.

Hambleden Mill;
Hambleden Marina

☆ Hambleden Lock

1½ miles

**R i v e r    T h a m e s**

2 miles

**3** ➤ **Cross** carefully at fingerpost and go between cottages.
➤ Emerge on lane and bear **right**.

**4** ➤ Pass to **right** of Hambleden Mill Marina's entrance, cross footbridge over weir and then cross lock gate.
➤ Bear **left**, quickly joining track beside River Thames and walk to next fork.

# NATURE NOTES

The tracks at the start of the walk are lined by hedges containing elder, sycamore, bramble and field maple. If you spot red 'blisters' on these maple leaves, there's no need to be alarmed; these are maple leaf galls. They are produced by tiny mites that feed on the leaves. Although they are regarded as a pest, they are unlikely to cause serious damage to the tree.

Along the riverbank, you'll probably see thistle, ragwort, great willowherb and goldenrod (solidago) while mallards, mute swans and Canada geese live on the water. Watch too for Egyptian geese. As their name suggests, these unusual-looking birds are native to Africa. They were introduced to the UK in the 18th century and the wild populations that exist on the Thames today are descendants of the escapees from those original ornamental collections.

Mallard ducklings

Flower Pot, Aston

**7**

Hambleden Lock ☆

**Hambleden Mill;** Hambleden Marir ☆

3 miles

2½ miles

**River Thames**

**5** ➡ As track swings away from river, keep **left** to pass round side of fencepost and through kissing-gate to continue beside riverbank to gated footbridge.

**6** ➡ Go through kissing-gate to cross footbridge and turn **right** along Ferry Lane.
➡ In hamlet of Aston, turn **right** at Flower Pot pub.
➡ In 70 yards reach a track on right.

**Above**: great willowherb
**Below**: maple leaf galls

**Top left**: Egyptian goose
**Left**: mute swan

Stag and Huntsman
Church of St
Mary the Virgin

Skirmett Road car park
(100 yards right)    3½ miles   **8**    4 miles

Hambleden car park

**1** ➠ Go **right** along broad track. This winds its way back to river, rejoining outward route at **5**.
➠ Turn **left** here and retrace steps for 1 mile to return to kissing-gate at **1**.

**8** ➠ **Cross** straight over track after kissing-gate and go through kissing-gate opposite.
➠ Follow faint grass path, aiming just left of church tower ahead to meet next kissing-gate.

**9** ➠ Through this turn **right** along lane into Hambleden.
➠ Keep **right**, passing church on left.
➠ Bear **right** at next lane junction. Car park is on **right** after pub.

Walk 7 Hambleden   59

Opposite (clockwise):
View Café at the
Chilterns Gateway
Centre; Fox and
Hounds, Christmas
Common
This page (clockwise):
The Bounty near
Cookham; Flower Pot,
Aston; Henley-on-
Thames; Coombe Hill;
The Squirrel, Penn
Street

# RIVER THAMES
# AT COOKHAM

This walk starts with a tranquil stroll beside the tree- and wildflower-edged Fleet Ditch before heading out across Cock Marsh's open grassland to reach the River Thames. As you then follow the riverside path to Cookham, there's a chance to visit an unusual pub that can be reached only on foot or by boat. Call in at Cookham for lunch, or just coffee and cake, before the final short stroll back to where the walk started.

## OS information

⊕ SU 892853
Explorer 172

**Distance**
3.2 miles/5.2km

**Time**
1½ hours

**Start/Finish**
Cookham Moor

**Parking** SL6 9SB
National Trust Cookham Moor pay-and-display car park on B4447, ⅓ mile west of its junction with A4094

**Public toilets**
None

### Cafés/pubs
The Bounty pub after ❸; Cookham

### Terrain
Riverside paths; open grassland; pavements and surfaced paths through village. (The riverside paths and meadows sometimes flood in winter.)

### Hilliness
Level throughout

### Footwear
Spring/Autumn/ Winter 🥾
Summer 🥾

### 🚂 Public transport
Route starts ⅓ mile from Cookham Rise Railway Station. Bus service 37/37A, between High Wycombe and Maidenhead, stops at Cookham Rise and Cookham: arrivabus. co.uk

### ♿ Accessibility
••••••••••
Wheelchairs: kissing-gates at ❶ and ❸ may not be passable but Thames Path, in dry conditions only, from ❸ to end (steps at ❼ can be bypassed). Suitable for all-terrain pushchairs

### 🐕 Dogs Welcome
but keep on leads. No stiles

**Did you know?** It may seem counter-intuitive, but grazing by cattle, as carried out for centuries on Cock Marsh, is a good way of maintaining healthy grassland and heathland habitats. Because of the plants they eat and the way they eat them – by wrapping their tongues around them and pulling them up – cattle help increase diversity. Their trampling of the ground makes it harder for large, vigorous plants to grow, creating an improved chance of survival for more delicate plants.

**Local legend** The Kings Arms in Cookham (originally called the King's Head) dates from the 17th century and was home to a widow called Martha Spott. This enterprising woman minted her own currency solely for use in Cookham – the 'half tokens' were probably used by the hostelry's customers for gambling.

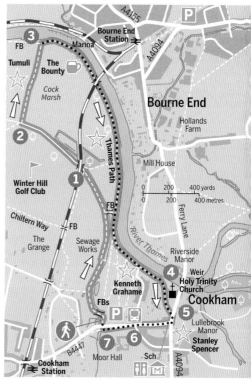

# STORIES BEHIND THE WALK

☆ **Kenneth Grahame** Born in Edinburgh, the author of the children's book *The Wind in the Willows* was raised by his grandparents in the nearby village of Cookham Dean from the age of five. Some of his famous novel is believed to have been inspired by his own experiences as he played on and around the River Thames as a child in the 1860s and 70s.

☆ **Thames Path** The Thames Path is a long-distance hiking trail that leads from the source of the river – in an unassuming meadow in the Cotswolds – to the Thames Barrier near Woolwich in south-east London. For 185 miles, it follows England's most famous river downstream, passing through London along the way. The Thames Path is one of 16 National Trails in England and Wales.

½ mile

Rail bri

Cookham Moor car park

➡ Walking away from road, take broad path to left of ticket machine.
➡ Just before gate into meadow, turn **left**, quickly crossing bridge.
➡ Walk with stream on right for ⅔ mile to T-junction just before railway bridge.

**1** ➡ At T-junction, turn **left**, through kissing-gate.
➡ Immediately after passing under railway, bear **right**, soon going through gate.
➡ After next gate, walk 300 yards on raised embankment along edge of Cock Marsh to boardwalk.

☆ **Tumuli** The four man-made hillocks, or tumuli, on Cock Marsh are burial mounds dating back to the Bronze Age. During a Victorian archaeological excavation of one of the larger mounds, the remains of a woman were found as well as what appeared to be a feast. One of the smaller tumuli contained the remains of a child. The nature of the burials suggests they were members of an important local family.

## ☆ Stanley Spencer

The artist Sir Stanley Spencer was born in Cookham in 1891 and lived there for most of his life. An official war artist during World War I, some of his most famous works are the murals in Sandham Memorial Chapel in Burghclere, Hampshire, which depict scenes from the battlefield and the home front. In 1950 he was awarded a CBE and he was knighted a year before his death in December 1959. The gallery in Cookham houses some of his artwork as well as personal effects.

The Bounty

Boardwalk   ☆ Tumuli

1 mile

C o c k   M a r s h

1½ miles

**2** ➡ Turn **right** along short section of boardwalk.
➡ When this ends, **continue** in same direction, later passing to right of prominent mound (tumulus) to meet riverbank.

**3** ➡ Reaching Thames just left of riverside properties, turn **right** through kissing-gate.
➡ Walk riverside path for 1⅓ miles, passing The Bounty pub and under railway, ultimately reaching property with high brick wall, 150 yards before main road bridge.

# NATURE NOTES

The first part of the walk follows the route of Fleet Ditch, the banks of which are home to trees and shrubs such as white willow, rowan, elder, bramble, hawthorn and oak. Growing along the edges of the stream itself, you might see purple loosestrife and great reedmace. Also known as bulrushes, the distinctive, sausage-shaped flowerheads of the great reedmace appear in the height of summer.

Cock Marsh is common land and has been grazed for centuries. The presence of commoners' cattle here allows wildflowers to flourish, including several species of orchid, wild thyme, meadow buttercup and the rare brown galingale, found in only 12 locations in the whole of Britain.

As on all the walks in this book, keep your eyes peeled for red kites. You might see them just about anywhere on the route.

**Top**: purple loosestrife
**Above**: meadow buttercup

R i v e r    T h a m e s

Railway bridge          2 miles

☆    T h a m e s    P a t h

**4** ➤ Go **right** at fingerpost, walking with wall on left.
➤ Go **straight over** crossing of paths in churchyard.
➤ Turn **left** along lane (Church Gate) to main road.

**5** ➤ Turn **right** at main road (A4094).
➤ Take next road on **right** (B4447), walking past shops and businesses to edge of Cookham Moor.

**Top left**: cattle in the Thames at Cock Marsh
**Above**: great reedmace
**Left**: bramble flowers

Kenneth
☆ Grahame
Holy Trinity Church
☆ Stanley Spencer
Steps (ramp close by)

2½ miles
Holy Trinity Church
3 miles
Cookham Moor **P**
car park

**6** ➤ Reaching edge of Cookham Moor, join broad, asphalt path to **left** of road. (White barrier across start of it.)
➤ Follow this for 230 yards to a flight of steps.

**7** ➤ Descend steps on **right** just before bridge over Fleet Ditch. (Steps can be avoided by continuing for few paces and using stony path instead.)
➤ **Cross** road to re-enter car park.

# WALK 9

# HENLEY-ON-THAMES

Henley-on-Thames is an attractive, fashionable and popular little town, sitting on the Oxfordshire bank of the river. This walk starts by immediately crossing to the Berkshire side and climbing gently through woodland and over fields with views out across this beautiful part of the Thames Valley. It then drops to Remenham, home to a pretty church, to begin the gentle stroll back to Henley beside England's most famous river.

During Regatta Week racing (first week of July), the route ❼ to ❽ is temporarily closed.

## OS information

🧭 SU 599806
Explorer 171

**Distance**
3.5 miles/5.6km

**Time**
2 hours

**Start/Finish**
Henley-on-Thames
Railway Station

**Parking** RG9 1AY
Railway station car
park; plenty of other
car parks in town

**Public toilets**
Opposite station

**Cafés/pubs**
Henley-on-Thames

**Terrain**
Pavement through
town; meadows,
fields and woodland
trails; quiet country
lanes; surfaced
riverside path.
(Thames Path
sometimes floods in
winter)

**Hilliness**
Undulating from ❷
to ❺, otherwise flat

**Footwear**
Winter 🥾
Spring/Summer/
Autumn 👟

**Local legend** Various locations around Henley, including the Little Angel pub, are said to be haunted by the ghost of Mary Blandy. She was hanged in 1752 for the murder of her father, Francis Blandy, the town clerk and a prominent lawyer. At her trial, she claimed she'd never intended to kill him; she'd believed the poison she'd given him to be a 'love potion' that would soften his heart to the man she wanted to marry.

**Public transport**
Rail services to Henley-on-Thames: southwesternrailway. com. Henley also has bus links with Reading, Marlow and High Wycombe (service 800): arrivabus. co.uk; Maidenhead (service 239): thamesvalleybuses. com

**Accessibility**
Town and riverside paths suitable for all: ① to ②, and ⑥ to end

**Dogs** Welcome but keep on leads. Three stiles (one leading into Remenham Woods soon after ③ does not have a dog gate)

**Did you know?** The Henley Royal Regatta started life in 1839 as a public fair with various attractions. Boat races had been taking place in the area for some time, and it was decided to formalise this. The focus quickly shifted from public amusement to competitive rowing, and it is now one of Britain's most famous boating events. It takes place over six days, usually ending the first weekend in July.

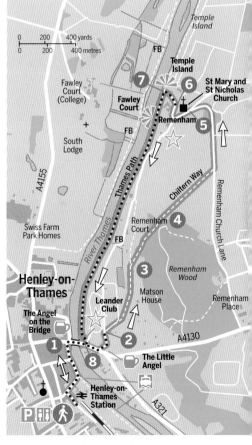

# STORIES BEHIND
# THE WALK

☆**Leander Club** Established in 1818, the Leander Club is one of the world's oldest rowing clubs. It is also one of the most prestigious, with members including Sir Steve Redgrave, Sir Matthew Pinsent, Peter Reed and James Cracknell, all winners of multiple Olympic gold medals. It was originally based in London, on the tidal stretch of the river, but moved its clubhouse to Henley in 1897.

**Fawley Court** The grand Fawley Court was built in 1684 for William Freeman, a slave owner who had plantations in St Ki and Montserrat. It is said that William of Orange stayed here in 1688 on his march t London, having landed with his army on the Devon coast to overthrow the Catholic kir James II. The house and grounds are said to be the inspiration for Toad Hall in Kenneth Grahame's *The Wind in the Willows*.

The Angel on
the Bridge

River
Thames

Henley
Bridge

  The Little Angel

½ mile

**P**
Railway
Station
car park

➤ With your back to station, turn **right** along road and **right** again at junction.
➤ Reaching River Thames, go **left** on riverside path.
➤ Nearing Angel on the Bridge pub, join pavement to left of it to main road.

**1** ➤ Go **right** at crossroads and use pedestrian crossing.
➤ Continue over river on road bridge.
➤ With Little Angel pub on corner, turn **left** along Remenham Lane for 170 yards to kissing-gate.

**Temple Island** The ornamental folly on Temple Island was built in the 1770s as a fishing lodge for the inhabitants and guests of Fawley Lodge. The starting point for the races of the Henley Royal Regatta, a 999-year lease of the island was purchased in 1987 by the regatta stewards, who then set about restoring the folly. It can be hired for weddings and other events, and, during the regatta, guests pay more than £500 each for this most exclusive of viewing areas.

☆ **Remenham** The name 'Remenham' means either 'Raven's home' of 'Home of the Remi', the latter being a Celtic tribe originating from northern France. In the mid-11th century, the manor was held by Queen Edith, Queen of England, and it was included among the King's lands during the Domesday survey later that same century. Most of the population was wiped out by the plague in 1664.

1 mile
**4**
Remenham Wood

1½ miles
**5**

**2** ➤ Turn **right** through kissing-gate in hedge.
➤ Walk along track; where it bends left, keep **ahead** to cross stile.
➤ Bear **left** over open ground then cross stile at top of short slope, passing through woodland.

**3** ➤ Emerging from trees, pass round side of gate. Bear **right**, steeply uphill on faint trail towards Remenham Woods.
➤ Cross stile and follow path all the way through woods.

# NATURE NOTES

**Above**: orange balsam
**Opposite**: **top**, red kite;
**middle**, yellow
loosestrife;
**bottom**, mint

The first part of the walk follows a series of trails through patches of woodland. Among the species you might see are elder, hawthorn, holly, sycamore, beech and ash.

Riverside plants are more likely to grab your attention on the second half of the walk, particularly in summer when their flowers bring a variety of colours to the banks of the Thames. Look for mint, yellow loosestrife and purple loosestrife. Orange balsam can be seen too. Like its better-known cousin, Himalayan balsam, this was brought into Britain as an ornamental plant and aggressively displaces native species.

It's common to see red kites in the skies over Henley and Remenham. These graceful birds of prey, with their distinctive forked tails, became extinct in England and Scotland in the second half of the 19th century but were successfully reintroduced in several areas, including the Chilterns, in the late 1980s and early 1990s.

St Mary and
St Nicholas
✝ Church

Temple Island

2 miles

Fawley Court

⑥ ⑦

☆ Remenham

R i v e r    T h a m e s

2½ miles

④ ▶ Leaving trees, **continue** in same direction, uphill on path through middle of field.
▶ Go through hedge gap and turn **left** along road. Follow it downhill, round **left** bend to junction.

⑤ ▶ Turn **left** at T-junction. Walk along road for 130 yards to junction.
▶ Go **right** (church on corner) to lane end at Remenham Manor.

⑥ ▶ When surfaced lane ends, keep **ahead**, passing round side of large gate.
▶ After next gate, cross rough track and go through another gate to river.

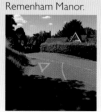

Canada goose, gulls and terns looking down river towards Temple Island

Leander Club

The Angel on the Bridge

3½ miles

3 miles

Henley Bridge

River Thames

P

Railway Station car park

**7** ➡ Turn **left** along surfaced riverside path.
➡ Walk beside river for slightly over 1 mile to brick wall of the Leander Club near Henley Bridge.

**8** ➡ Pass in front of Leander Club and follow enclosed path **left**.
➡ At junction with main road, turn **right** to recross road bridge.
➡ Use pedestrian crossing and return to station.

# RIVER THAMES
# AT GORING

Goring is a picturesque village located in one of the loveliest stretches of the Thames Valley – where the rolling Chiltern Hills meet the farmed uplands of the North Wessex Downs. After leaving the village, this walk follows a series of easy-going tracks out into the pretty countryside. Beyond the tranquil hamlet of Gatehampton Manor, it joins the Thames Path for a relaxing riverside stroll back to Goring where a choice of pubs and cafés await the tired walker.

| OS information | |
|---|---|
| SU 763822 Explorer 171 | |
| **Distance** | 3 miles/4.8km |
| **Time** | 1½ hours |
| **Start/Finish** | Goring |
| **Parking** RG8 9HB | Wheel Orchard pay-and-display car park, Goring |
| **Public toilets** | In car park |
| **Cafés/pubs** | Goring |
| **Terrain** | Village roads and pavements; rough tracks; riverside paths and meadow. (Thames Path sometimes floods in winter.) |
| **Hilliness** | Level apart from gentle slopes on approach to and departure from river |
| **Footwear** | Winter 🥾 Spring/Summer/Autumn 👟 |

**Did you know?** Goring lies on the south-western edge of the Chilterns Area of Outstanding Natural Beauty (AONB). Recognised for their exceptional landscapes, there are 46 AONBs in England, Wales and Northern Ireland, each of which receives a degree of statutory protection. The area on the other side of the River Thames lies within the North Wessex Downs AONB.

**Local legend** Goring Lock was the scene of a tragedy in July 1674 when 60 people drowned in a ferry accident. They were returning to Streatley on the Berkshire side of the river, having attended the annual 'Goring Feast'. According to local reports at the time, the ferryman rowed too close to the weir and the packed boat was overturned by the force of the water.

### Public transport

Route starts ¼ mile from Goring & Streatley Railway Station; bus service 134 to Goring from Wallingford: goingforwardbuses.com

### Accessibility

Village sections suitable for wheelchairs – 🚶 to almost ② and ⑦ to end; all-terrain pushchairs throughout, although there is a width-restricting barrier between ① and ②

### Dogs

Welcome but keep on leads. No stiles

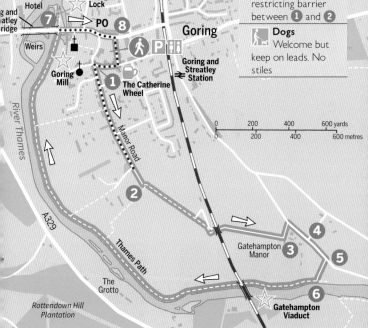

# STORIES BEHIND THE WALK

☕ **The Catherine Wheel** Probably built in the 1660s, the Catherine Wheel is the oldest pub in Goring. It became part of the estate of Henry Allnutt, a London lawyer who established a charity that built almhouses and a school for the area's poor. The adjacent building was the village smithy and wheelwright. It wasn't unusual for customers to sit and enjoy a beer while their horses were being shod.

☆ **Gatehampton Viaduct**

This viaduct consists of two parallel railway bridges. The first, designed by the famous engineer Isambard Kingdom Brunel, was built in 1840 to carry the Great Western Railway across the River Thames on its way from London to the south-west of England. The second 'relief' bridge was built in the 1890s to increase capacity on the line. The viaduct is now a Grade II-listed structure.

☕ The Catherine Wheel

**P** Wheel Orchard car park   M a n o r   R o a d   ½ mile

**1** ➤ Take next road on **left** – Manor Road.
➤ Continue **straight ahead** when it becomes rough track, later passing round side of gate across track to junction.

➤ Leave car park via vehicle entrance.
➤ At end of access lane turn **right** onto Station Road.

## ☆ Goring Mill

The water mill that exists beside the River Thames in Goring today was built in the 18th century, although it is thought there has been one in this area since before the Norman Conquest. The landscape artist JMW Turner painted the mill in the early years of the 19th century. The work, although never completed, is now part of the Tate Britain collection.

## ☆ Goring Lock

Like Hambleden Lock (page 56), the lock at Goring started life as a flash lock. It was built, probably during the reign of Henry VIII, to enable the local miller to control the flow of water to his mill, and it also made navigation easier. The first pound lock was constructed in 1787, made from local oak and based on a similar design to the one that exists today but with a pair of gates in the middle of it.

Gatehampton Manor ·····③······ ④

Railway bridge     ¦1 mile     ⑤

⑥

1½ miles ¦

**②** ► Keep **left** as another track goes right.
► Follow route round sharp bends to **left** and **right**, and under railway.
► Pass round side of gate to keep **straight on** along track for 325 yards to Gatehampton Manor.

**③** ► Having passed first set of buildings at Gatehampton Manor, turn **left** at crossing of surfaced routes.
► After 70 yards, take track on **right**, with Pip's Barn on the corner, walking to next crossways.

# NATURE NOTES

The verges and hedgerows lining the tracks followed on the first part of this walk are full of life in spring, summer and autumn. You'll see hawthorn, small oak trees, ash, bramble and traveller's joy (clematis). In winter, the wispy, white seed heads of this clematis cover the hedgerows, giving rise to the plant's alternative name, old man's beard. Watch too for the striking blue flowers of chicory.

The Thames-side meadows and riverbanks are home to great willowherb, ragwort, dog rose, and meadow cranesbill, as well as various trees and shrubs; these include willow, sycamore, hawthorn, horse chestnut, elder and blackthorn.

The most common birds seen on the water include mute swan, heron and Canada goose. Hedgerow birds to look out for are chaffinch, greenfinch, and the more secretive bullfinch and whitethroat.

Among the fish regularly caught in the Thames downstream of Goring weirs are roach, chub, dace, bream, perch and pike.

Greenfinch

☆ Gatehampton Viaduct

2 miles

R i v e r   T h a m e s

**4** ➡ Here, go **straight over**, passing between cottage (on right) and garage.
➡ Continue on track for 120 yards to Thames Path junction.

**5** ➡ Take enclosed path on **right**, following Thames Path down to a small bridge in front of the river.

**6** ➡ After small bridge, turn **right**.
➡ Follow riverside path for 1½ miles, passing under railway viaduct, all the way to Goring and Streatley Bridge.

**Top left**: heron
**Top right**: whitethroat
**Above**: chicory
**Left**: traveller's joy

i v e r   T h a m e s

Goring Lock ☆

Goring Mill ☆

3 miles

P

Goring and
Streatley Bridge

Wheel Orchard
car park

2½ miles

**7** ➡ Turn **right** just before bridge over Thames.
➡ Path broadens to become lane. Continue **straight on**, soon joining pavement.
➡ **Cross** Manor Road to continue on High Street through village to next right turning.

**8** ➡ Turn sharp **right** immediately after row of shops and businesses (signed Library).
➡ Follow fenced path back into car park.

## Publishing information

© Crown copyright 2023.
All rights reserved.

Ordnance Survey, OS, and the OS logos are registered trademarks, and OS Short Walks Made Easy is a trademark of Ordnance Survey Ltd.

© Crown copyright and database rights (2023) Ordnance Survey.

ISBN 978 0 319092 62 0
1st edition published by Ordnance Survey 2023.

www.ordnancesurvey.co.uk

While every care has been taken to ensure the accuracy of the route directions, the publishers cannot accept responsibility for errors or omissions, or for changes in details given. The countryside is not static: hedges and fences can be removed, stiles can be replaced by gates, field boundaries can alter, footpaths can be rerouted and changes in ownership can result in the closure or diversion of some concessionary paths. Also, paths that are easy and pleasant for walking in fine conditions may become slippery, muddy and difficult in wet weather.

If you find an inaccuracy in either the text or maps, please contact Ordnance Survey at os.uk/contact.

A catalogue record for this book is available from the British Library.

## Milestone Publishing credits

**Author**: Vivienne Crow

**Series editor**: Kevin Freeborn

**Maps**: Cosmographics

**Design and Production**: Patrick Dawson, Milestone Publishing

Printed in India by Replika Press Pvt. Ltd

## Photography credits

**Front cover**: Joe Dunckley/Shutterstock.com. **Back cover** cornfield/Shutterstock.com.

All photographs supplied by the author ©Vivienne Crow except page 6 Karl Rushen and pages 25, 38, 39, 47 Kevin Freeborn.

The following images were supplied by Shutterstock.com: pages 1 Chrislofotos; 18 Sokolov Alexey; 24 F.Neidl; 24 Alec Issigonis; 24 Rory Glanville; 25 Jonas Vegele; 26 kentaylordesign; 33 Sandra Standbridge; 33 Stefan Rotter; 33 Pdsfotografie; 38 Bildagentur Zoonar GmbH; 39 IanRedding; 40 Anna_Borowska; 40 Amanda Jayne Smith; 41 Karl Weller; 47 Simon Bratt; 52 Paulius Beinaravicius; 52 Vastram; 58 Andy119; 60, 70 Colin Burdett; 73 Rusana Krasteva; 78, 79 SanderMeertinsPhotography.